Introduction

Have you ever wondered why the sky turns different colors? Let's ask science about this! There are wavelengths all around us and these waves exist of frequencies known as the Electromagnetic Spectrum. Diagram 1 shows both the Electromagnetic and Visible Light Spectrum. The Visible Light Spectrum is the electromagnetic waves humans are able to see. The "light" we see is called ROYGBV and stands for; Red, Orange, Yellow, Green, Blue and Violet. When you see all these together it forms the non-color white. When these waves are absent then you see the non-color black.

The Sun produces these wavelengths making us see "white" light. However, a variety of disruptions in the atmosphere block some of the ROYGBV. Gases such as Oxygen and Nitrogen can knock some of the colors away. Gases from plants or pollution all play a part in the changing of the sky colors. Atmospheric particles mostly alter the high frequencies blue and violet, leaving the lower frequencies red, orange and yellow to be more present. Since the sun setting is further away than the sun in the daytime, more of the red, orange and yellow colors will be seen. Our eyes are more sensitive to blue frequencies and this is why we see a blue sky.

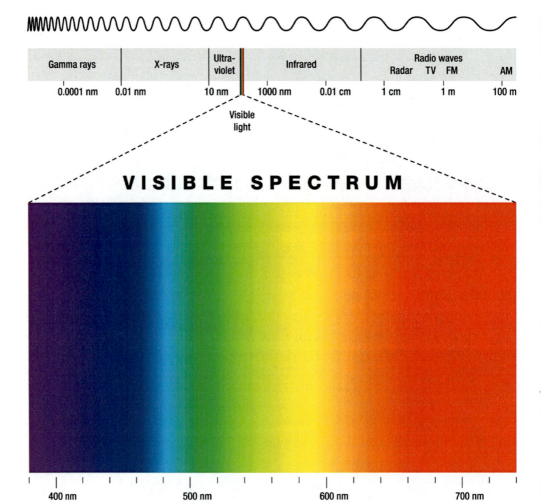

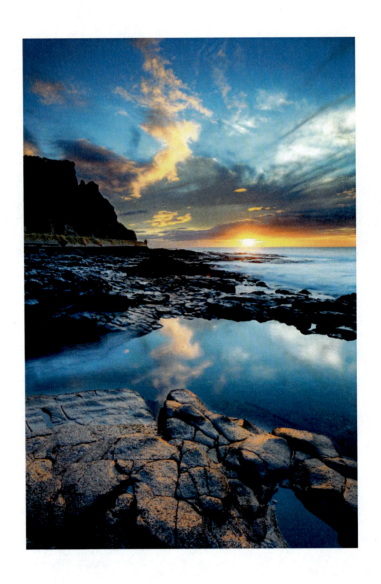

All Rights Reserved. No part of this publication may be reproduced in any form or by any means, including electronic transfer, scanning, photocopying, or otherwise without prior written permission of the copyright holder. Copyright 2014 Smooth

Made in the USA
San Bernardino, CA
19 December 2016